This book belongs to:

____

24 23 22 21 1 2 3 4

Published by Tughra Books
335 Clifton Ave.
Clifton, NJ, 07011, USA
www.tughrabooks.com

ISBN: 979-8-89729-502-9

Mini Muslims Series ISBN 9781597849692

WHO IS Muhammad (pbuh)

Allah revealed His message to certain people
in order to teach us about Him
and how to worship Him.

These people are called prophets.

Prophets taught us that Allah is the One True God.

They showed us what is right and wrong.

Muhammad (pbuh) is the last prophet.

His message of Islam is for everyone.

After we say his name we always say

"peace be upon him".

Allah sent down the Quran through him.

The Quran is the exact words of Allah.

Prophet Muhammad (pbuh)

taught people about Allah.

He taught us that Allah is One, that He is our Creator, and that He is the Most Merciful.

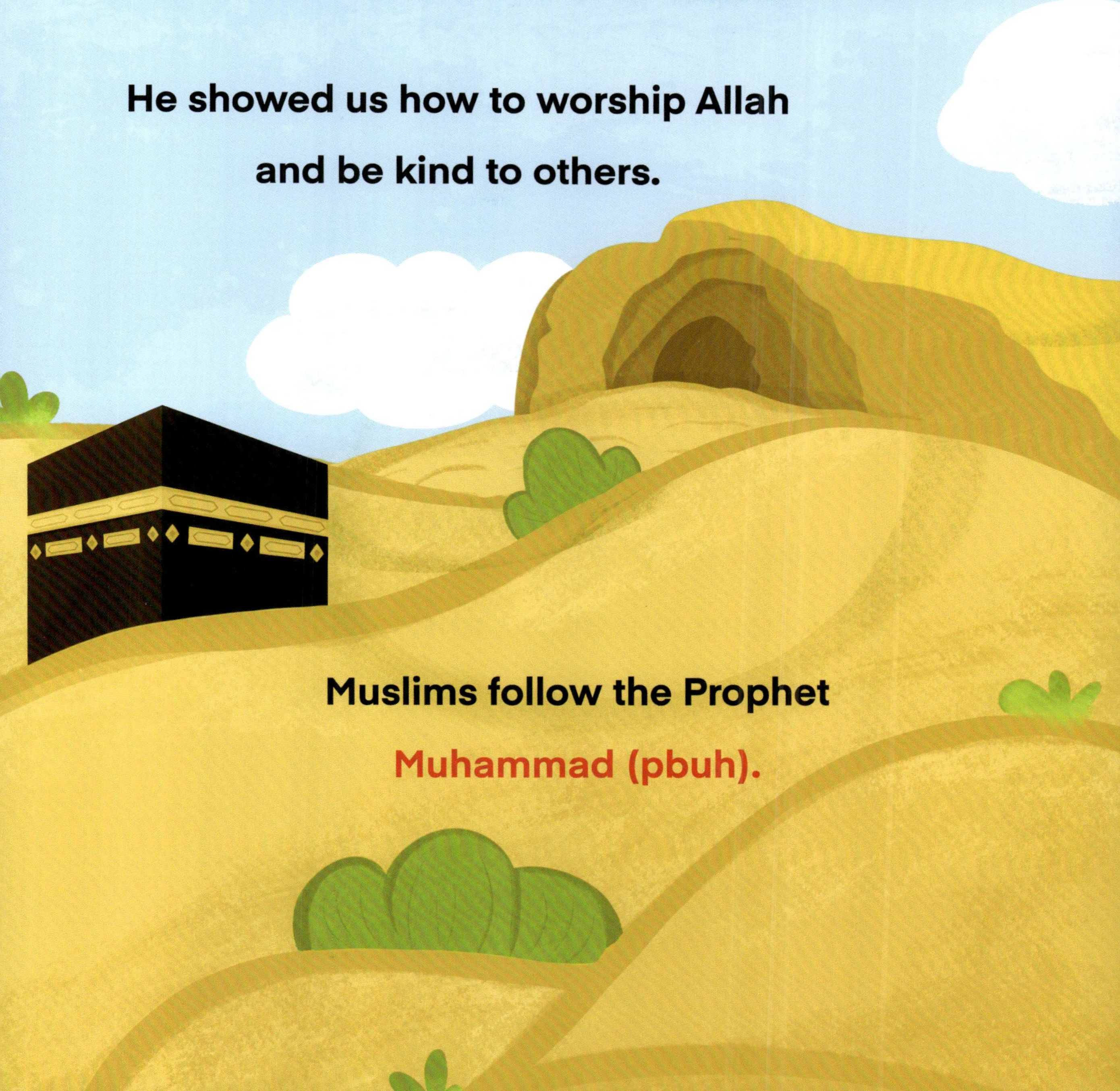

He showed us how to worship Allah

and be kind to others.

Muslims follow the Prophet

Muhammad (pbuh).

He was honest, kind, caring, smart
and brave. He was a mercy to the world.

He was a prophet, a leader, a father
a husband, a teacher, and a friend.

Prophet Muhammad (pbuh)
loves us and we love him!

I ♥
Mohammed
(PBUH)